First World War
and Army of Occupation
War Diary
France, Belgium and Germany

4 CAVALRY DIVISION
Divisional Troops
Divisional Sanitary Section
1 January 1917 - 21 March 1918

WO95/1158/8

The Naval & Military Press Ltd
www.nmarchive.com
Published in association with The National Archives

Published by

The Naval & Military Press Ltd

Unit 10 Ridgewood Industrial Park,

Uckfield, East Sussex,

TN22 5QE England

Tel: +44 (0) 1825 749494

www.naval-military-press.com

www.nmarchive.com

This diary has been reprinted in facsimile from the original. Any imperfections are inevitably reproduced and the quality may fall short of modern type and cartographic standards.

© **Crown Copyright**
Images reproduced by permission of The National Archives, London, England, 2015.

Contents

Document type	Place/Title	Date From	Date To
Heading	WO95/1158/8		
Heading	1918 4th Cavalry Division 4th Cav. Sanitary Section 1917 Jan-1918 Mar To Egypt 4 Cav Div		
Heading	War Diary of Captain C.R. O'Brien Indian Medical Service Officer Commanding 4th Cavalry Sanitary Section From 1st January to 31st January 1917 (Volume XX)		
War Diary	Fressennville	01/01/1917	31/01/1917
Heading	Sanitary Section, 4th. Cav Div. Feb 1917		
Heading	War Diary of Captain C.R. O'Brien Indian Medical Service Officer Commanding 4th Cavalry Sanitary Sectors From 1st February 1917 to 28th Fabruary (Volume XXI)		
War Diary	Fressennville	01/02/1917	28/02/1917
Heading	Sanitary Section-4th Cav Div. March 1917		
Heading	War Diary of Captain C.R. O'Brien Indian Medical Service Officer Commanding 4th Cavalry Sanitary Section from 1st March 1917 to 31st March 1917 (Volume XXII)		
War Diary	Fressennville	01/03/1917	29/03/1917
War Diary	Albert	30/03/1917	31/03/1917
Heading	Sanitary Section-4th Cav Div. April 1917		
Heading	War Diary of Capt C.R. O'Brien Indian Medical Service O.B. 4th Cavalry Sanitary Section from 1st April 1917 to 30th April 1917 (Volume XXIII)		
War Diary	Albert	01/04/1917	19/04/1917
War Diary	Marieux	20/04/1917	30/04/1917
Heading	4th. Cav. Div. Sanitary Section May 1917-June 1917		
Heading	War Diary of Captain C.R. O'Brien Indian Medical Service Officer Commanding 4th Cavalry Sanitary Section from 1st May 1917 to 31st May 1917 (Volume XXIV)		
War Diary	Marieux	01/05/1917	15/05/1917
War Diary	Fougques	16/05/1917	31/05/1917
Heading	War Diary of Captain C.R. O'Brien Indian Medical Service Officer Commanding 4th Cavalry Sanitary Section from 1st jun 1917 to 30th jun 1917 (Volume XXV)		
War Diary	Fourques	01/06/1917	30/06/1917
Heading	San Sect-4th Cav Div. June1917		
Heading	War Diary of Captain C.R. O'Brien Indian Medical Service Officer Commanding 4th Cavalry Sanitary Section from 1st July 1917 to 31 July 1917 (Volume XXVI)		
War Diary	Fourques	01/07/1917	31/07/1917
Heading	4th Cav. Div. San Sect Aug 1917		
Heading	War Diary of Captain C.R. O'Brien Indian Medical Service Officer Commanding 4th Cavalry Sanitary Section from 1st August 1917 to 31st August 1917 (Volume XXVII)		

War Diary	Fourques	01/08/1917	31/08/1917
Heading	4th Cav. Div. Sanitary Section Sept 1917		
Heading	War Diary of Captain C.R. O'Brien Indian Medical Service Officer Commanding 4th Cavalry Sanitary Section from 1st Sept 1917 to 30 Sept 1917 (Volume XXVIII)		
War Diary	Fourques	01/10/1917	30/10/1917
Heading	4th Cav. Sanitary Section Oct 1917		
Heading	War Diary of Captain C.R. O'Brien Indian Medical Service Officer Commanding 4th Cavalry Sanitary Section from 1st October 1917 to 31st October 1917 (Volume XXIX)		
War Diary	Fourques	01/10/1917	31/10/1917
Heading	4th Cav. Sanitary Section Nov 1917		
Heading	War Diary of Captain C.R. O'Brien Indian Medical Service Officer Commanding 4th Cavalry Sanitary Section from 1st December 1917 to 30th December (Volume XXX)		
War Diary	Fourques	01/11/1917	30/11/1917
Heading	War Diary of Captain C.R. O'Brien Indian Medical Service Officer Commanding 4th Cavalry Sanitary Section from 1st December to 31st December 1917 (Volume XXXI)		
War Diary	Fourques	01/12/1917	31/12/1917
Heading	War Diary of Capt C.R. O'Brien I.M.S. Officer Commanding 4th Cavalry Sanitary Section from 1st January 1918 to 31st January 1918 (Volume XXXII)		
War Diary	Fourques	01/01/1918	31/01/1918
Heading	War Diary of Officer Cammanding 4th Cavalry Sanitary Section from 1st February 1918 to 28th February 1918 (Volume XXXIII)		
War Diary	Fourques	01/02/1918	07/02/1918
War Diary	Saleux	08/02/1918	28/02/1918
War Diary	Poix	01/03/1918	21/03/1918

No 95/11 58/8

1918
4TH CAVALRY DIVISION

4TH CAV. SANITARY SECTION

~~JAN - MAR 1918~~

1917 JAN — 1918 MAR

To EGYPT 4 CAV. DIV

(Original copy in January 1917)

Army Form C. 2118.

Serial No. 296.

WAR DIARY
or
INTELLIGENCE SUMMARY.
(Erase heading not required.)

Place	Date	Hour	Summary of Events and Information	Remarks and references to Appendices

(SECRET)

War Diary
of
Captain C.R. O'BRIEN, Acting M.O. 5th
Officer Commanding 4th Cavalry Sanitary Section.

From 1st January 1917 .... to 31st January 1917.

(Prine II.)

COMMITTEE FOR THE
MEDICAL HISTORY OF THE WAR
Date 23 APR. 1917

WAR DIARY
or
INTELLIGENCE SUMMARY.

(Erase heading not required.)

Army Form C. 2118.

Place	Date	Hour	Summary of Events and Information	Remarks and references to Appendices
FRESSENNEVILLE	1st January 1917		New Years day. Self & head gunner at ST VALERY to see the A.D.M.S. Saw men of the Indian infantry working at the JODHPUR C.F.A at the dent dump at WOINCOURT. their infantry working at the JODHPUR dumps, there day, with Lloyd Scoggs	
"	2nd January		VALINES. Saw the JODHPUR dumps. there day, with Lloyd Scoggs. to CHEPPY to see the M.O. 29th Lancers also L. BOUBERT where I saw the Mo AMBALLA C.F.A Section in billets. Visited all day. their infantry working at VALINES	
"	3rd January		testine in billets. Self to QUESNOY-LE-MONTANT when I saw the M.O. 36th Jacobs Horse. Proceeded to visit the two infantry there in the 8th + 9th Lake to CHEPPY where the two infantry were working. I also inspected billets & found when of an sympathies there. thought much need dong so	did
"	4th January		to ARREST to see the M.O. 6th Cavalry. also inspected billets & installation of an sympathies there also inspected working in the afternoon for the O.O.S. Remained all day	did
"	5th January		to ST VALERY where I saw the D.A.D.M.S. two infantry working for the E.C.S. Section on a road trench	did

WAR DIARY
or
INTELLIGENCE SUMMARY.
(Erase heading not required.)

Army Form C. 2118.

Place	Date	Hour	Summary of Events and Information	Remarks and references to Appendices
FRESSENVILLE	6th January		Taken on a route march in the morning. Left L. ST VALERY in a number of 4-horse transports. P.8 men like 6. FRANLEU of 15 the three prisoners	
"	7th January		Sunday — taken in billets. Left L. CHEPPY to be the H/Q 29th hussars. Left L. ACHEUX to be the H/Q LUCKNOW C.F.A Received orders to visit and NCO & 13 men L. CAYEUX to make known standings for the drive, round Central Bright	
"	6th January		with day. 13 men & 1 NCO L. CAYEUX as ordered. Left L. SAKENELLE when I inspected billet demolition of A Battery QHA also arranged to visit the divisional lines — the 10th Lke. UL L. ARREST when I saw the 9th. 6th Cavalry div. and visited at CHEPPY marking for the 29th Hussars	
"	9th January		division inspection at ACHEUX marking UT LUCKNOW C.F.A. attending thereon. I have now throughout the QHO clay boot and go out.	

Army Form C. 2118.

WAR DIARY
or
INTELLIGENCE SUMMARY.
(Erase heading not required.)

Place	Date	Hour	Summary of Events and Information	Remarks and references to Appendices
FRESSENVILLE	10th January		Le QUESNOY-LE-MONTANT to see the M.O. 3．．8．H. Jocks Horse to arrange for the use of the rifle ranges for the regiment. His infantry at SALENELLE where I saw musketry for A Battery R.H.A. which had just returned from the front.	
"	11th January		His infantry to ARREST to meet Major Ahmad, M.G., of the 6th Cavalry. Left to OFFEUX to see the M.O. MHOW Brigade M.G.S. in a case of diphtheria which had occurred there. Later to see the A.D.M.S. at Headquarters.	
"	12th January		His infantry to 3．．8．H. Jocks Horse at QUESNOY-LE-MONTANT about R.D.M. a Sowar reviewed between Sowar of my Indian Personnel having N.C.O.s of the E.O.S. who complained of having been assaulted. Held an immediate also his case which proved unable to reveal. 2 men who were identified were placed under arrest.	

Army Form C. 2118.

WAR DIARY
or
INTELLIGENCE SUMMARY.
(Erase heading not required.)

Place	Date	Hour	Summary of Events and Information	Remarks and references to Appendices
FRESSENVILLE	13 January		Two inspections at MIANNAY - working for the 1/2 R.D.C. held another when the scheme for use in the event of an air raid entailed their withdrawal in the event of enemy troops was rehearsed by the Brigade. N.C.O's having been one of the period another ... the ... D.O.M.S. & D.A.D.O.S. Lieut gardein shewn & St BLIMONT where I saw the round where there on the 13th & 16th and the A.D.M.T. arranged to have Lieuten KRISHNA SWAMY placed at their garden the following day 2 N/10 2/9 th Lancers knowing him at MIANNAY.	
,,	14 ,, January		Long walk Lieutenan KRISHNA SWAMY & a friend to ST VALERY to propose the A.D.M. came in & the long interval at midnight without his inclines having him covered and him up later to QUESNOY - LE - MONTANT when the inspection was completed on the 28th January 1 imperial Service Horse left in the morning & N.B.A.S. where 1 imperial Cavalry shewn whilst 1/2	
,,	15 ,, January		Signature of the 36th C.I.H commenced on morning	

WAR DIARY
or
INTELLIGENCE SUMMARY

Army Form C. 2118.

Place	Date	Hour	Summary of Events and Information	Remarks and references to Appendices
FRESSENVILLE	16th January		Two inspections to CHEPPY & took (in the 29th Lancers Sowars KRISHNASWAMY received 12 slight wounds the arm at the E.B.S. left L. BOUBERT to see the M.O. SIALKOTE C.F.A but diphtheria the 6th Cavalry. they were arranged to bring the two inspected to syphil. ARREST in the 19th & 29th	
"	17th January		to MHOW Bungalo at OFFEUX where I saw the A.D.M.S. later to CAYEUX to see the 19th Lancers two inspections at ST BLIMONT looking for the 17th Lancers	
"	18th January		two inspections again to the 17th Lancers left to CAYEUX Indian 1 small she supplied during round School examining	
"	19th January		two inspections to 6th Cavalry at ARREST left L'OFFEUX where a pretty man was inspecting a killed in hospital a case of syphilis had removed. Later to ARREST & on to SIALKOTE C.F.A. from thence to BOUBERT & on to SIALKOTE C.F.A.	

WAR DIARY
or
INTELLIGENCE SUMMARY
(Erase heading not required)

Army Form 2118.

Place	Date	Hour	Summary of Events and Information	Remarks and references to Appendices
FRESSENNEVILLE	20 January	4	The bus inspector having completed the work at ARREST worked in the afternoon for the SIALHOTE 2FA at BOUBERT turning my hand	Col. Brown eng/Comd
do	21 January	do	Sun day – nothing of note. bus inspector having the holds to shift cleaned and washed bought & found	
do	22 January	do	To CAYEUX to pay British stationer personnel attached to the divisional school. bus inspector working these to the CR 19 th lorries still passing my	
do	23 January	do	To ST BLIMONT where I inspected killed sanitation of the 17 th lancers the bus inspector completed work at CAYEUX	
do	24 January	do	To ARREST where I inspected killed sanitation of two squadrons of the 6th Cavalry. bus inspector to the workshops for monthly overhaul. still passing my hand	Col.
do	26 January	4	To ST BLIMONT where I completed sanitation of the village. bus inspector still at the workshops. turning hand in for monthly no problem	Col.

Army Form C. 2118.

WAR DIARY
or
INTELLIGENCE SUMMARY.
(Erase heading not required.)

Place	Date	Hour	Summary of Events and Information	Remarks and references to Appendices
FRESSENNVILLE	26/4 January		The dire infector returned from the workshops in the evening after having made four round trips returned by to BOUBERT to see the 4th RIANDTE C.F.A. freezing hard.	Syl Ref
Do.	27/4 January		L. DEHANCOURT where I inspected billets reindeer of two Squadrons of the O.I.H. Still freezing.	Ref
Do.	28/4 January		L. hand quarters where I saw the D.A.D.M.S. Bitterly cold.	Ref
Do.	29/4 January		Stayed indoors all day, as I was suffering from a bad cold. Hard freezing hard.	Ref
Do.	30/4 January		L. head quarters St. BLIMONT to see much for the 17th Lancers freezing hard.	Ref
Do.	31/4 January		Snow fell during the night. Sheer freezing - nothing of note.	Ref

Sanitary Sections, 4th Cav Div.

COMMITTEE FOR THE
MEDICAL HISTORY OF THE WAR
Date 21 MAY 1917

Army Form C. 2118.

WAR DIARY
or
INTELLIGENCE SUMMARY.
(Erase heading not required.)

(Original Copy)

Serial No. 296

SECRET.

War Diary
of
Captain C.R. O'BRIEN, Indian Medical Service
Officer Commanding No. 4 Cavalry Sanitary Section

From 1st February 1914 to 23rd February 1914

(Frame XVI)

Place	Date	Hour	Summary of Events and Information	Remarks and references to Appendices

WAR DIARY
or
INTELLIGENCE SUMMARY.
(Erase heading not required.)

Army Form C. 2118.

Original copy

Place	Date	Hour	Summary of Events and Information	Remarks and references to Appendices
FRESSENNVILLE	1st February 1917		1 l/cor Sergeant + 7 men to WOINCOURT for a month's duty under the Railhead supply officer. Freezing.	all fine weather
Do.	2nd February		Nothing to note.	do
Do.	3rd February		L/Cpl CROOK A.S.C. (MT) having been remanded was struck off the strength of the section.	do
Do.	4th February		Nothing to note.	do
Do.	5th Feb.			
Do.	6th Feb.		Private ROBBINS A.S.C. (MT) reported his arrival, was taken on the strength of the section.	do
Do.	7th " 8th " 9th " 10th "		nothing to note.	do

Army Form C. 2118.

WAR DIARY
or
INTELLIGENCE SUMMARY.

(Erase heading not required.)

Instructions regarding War Diaries and Intelligence Summaries are contained in F. S. Regs., Part II. and the Staff Manual respectively. Title pages will be prepared in manuscript.

Place	Date	Hour	Summary of Events and Information	Remarks and references to Appendices
FRESSENNVILLE	February			
	11th		} nothing to note. Every day to usual.	
	12th			
	13th			
	14th			
	15th			
	16th			
	17th		Troops JASU DOSS in advance to Hingh?	
D°	18th		} nothing to note.	
	19th			
	20th			
	21st			

WAR DIARY
or
INTELLIGENCE SUMMARY.

(Erase heading not required.)

Army Form C 2118.

Place	Date	Hour	Summary of Events and Information	Remarks and references to Appendices
FRESSENVILLE	22nd February		Lieuts. JASUDOSS having been transferred from Strength of the section	about Feb.
"	23rd Feb		nothing to note.	
"	24th Feb		Sergt. FENN R.A.M.C. with 12 men of the section reported from the divisional school	
"	25th "			
"	26th "		nothing to note.	
"	27th "			
"	28th "			

Sanitary Section — 4th Cav. Div.

COMMITTEE FOR THE
MEDICAL HISTORY OF THE WAR
Date -6 JUL.1917

(Original copy MARCH 1917)

Army Form C. 2118.

Serial No. 296

WAR DIARY
or
INTELLIGENCE SUMMARY.
(Erase heading not required.)

Summary of Events and Information

MEDICAL

SECRET

War Diary
of
Captain C.R. O'BRIEN, Indian Medical Service,
Officer Commanding 4th Darwa[?] Sanitary Section

From 1st March 1917 to 31st March 1917.

(Signed) C. R. O'Brien, Capt.

Original copy

WAR DIARY
or
INTELLIGENCE SUMMARY.
(Erase heading not required.)

(MARCH 1914)

Army Form C. 2118.

Place	Date	Hour	Summary of Events and Information	Remarks and references to Appendices
FRESSENNEVILLE	1st March		9 men into town detached for duty at Rushford returned to the unit	rifle rept. lost
"	2nd		} nothing to note	
"	3rd			
"	4th			
"	5th			
"	6th			rsd
"	7th March		1 sowar Lascha JOSEPH been revested to nothing Lascher in evening on his bushaw is killed.	rsd
"	8th March		Lascha BASANT. Promoted to 1 sowar Lascher vice JOSEPH degraded.	rsd
"	9th		} nothing to note.	
"	10th			
"	11th			rsd
"	12th			

Army Form C. 2118.

WAR DIARY
or
INTELLIGENCE SUMMARY.

(Erase heading not required.)

Instructions regarding War Diaries and Intelligence
Summaries are contained in F. S. Regs., Part II.
and the Staff Manual respectively. Title pages
will be prepared in manuscript.

Place	Date	Hour	Summary of Events and Information	Remarks and references to Appendices
FAEGENHUILLE	13.4	morn.	Am ordered to take command of JODHPUR I.F.A. in addition to my own duties. vice Capt. T.B. BOMFORD I.M.S. invalided to India	
do.	14.4			
do.	15.4		nothing to note	
do.	16.4			
do.	17.4			
do.	18.4		Sweepers JOSEPH evacuated sick & struck off the strength of the section.	
do.	19.4		Bikanir moved up to the 5th Army over behind up behind to clear up present area	
do.	20.4		nothing to note	
do.	21.4			
do.	22.4		Sweepers MAKBUL & DILAWAR evacuated sick & struck off the strength of the section.	

WAR DIARY
INTELLIGENCE SUMMARY

Place	Date	Hour	Summary of Events and Information	Remarks and references to Appendices
FRESSENVILLE	March 23rd		nothing to note	
"	24		Enemy in HEERA surrendered and advanced up the straight road	
"	25		} nothing to note	
"	26			
"	27			
"	28		Received orders by wire to despatch broken personnel with diminished men of division by train from ABBEVILLE. The party with 2 British N.C.O. left with by train for new area.	
"	29		left with remainder of section left by road for new area. Had to billet for the night at DROIEL.	

WAR DIARY
INTELLIGENCE SUMMARY

Place	Date	Hour	Summary of Events and Information	Remarks and references to Appendices
ALBERT	30th [month]		Section arrived and settled down in new billets.	
"	31st		Nothing to note.	

M. Power
Capt. RAMC
O.C. Mounted Sect.
4th Cavalry Division

Sanitary Station - 4th Cav Dis

April 1917

COMMITTEE FOR THE
MEDICAL HISTORY OF THE WAR
Date −6 JUL. 1917

Army Form C. 2118.

Original copy for April 1914

Serial No. 296.

WAR DIARY
or
INTELLIGENCE SUMMARY.
(Erase heading not required.)

"Medical."

Place	Date	Hour	Summary of Events and Information	Remarks and references to Appendices

(SECRET)

War Diary
of
Capt. C.P. O'BRIEN Adm Medical Service
O.C. 4th Mounted Brigade Sanitary Section
from 1st April 1914 to 30th April 1914
(Signed) XXIII

Army Form C. 2118.

WAR DIARY
or
INTELLIGENCE SUMMARY.
(Erase heading not required.)

Instructions regarding War Diaries and Intelligence Summaries are contained in F.S. Regs., Part II. and the Staff Manual respectively. Title pages will be prepared in manuscript.

Place	Date	Hour	Summary of Events and Information	Remarks and references to Appendices
ALBERT	1st April 1917		Sweepers M.T. 2017 BALJOUR arrived as reinforcement from the ell.	1
			" " 10 JWALI MASI	
			" " 2008 BHANTA	He has since taken on the
			" " 2060 MANGA	strength of the Section. Capt. Kn.
D°	2nd April		nothing to note.	Ref
D°	3rd April		Under instructions from the A.D.M.S. N.T. N°. 10 Sweeper JWALA MASI has been placed for duty with the AMBALLA	
			C.F.A. own detach of the strength of the Section.	
	4th April		⎫	
	5th "		⎪	
	6th "		⎪	
D°	7th "		⎬ nothing to note.	
	8th "		⎪	
	9th "		⎪	
	10th "		⎭	

Army Form C. 2118.

WAR DIARY
or
INTELLIGENCE SUMMARY.
(Erase heading not required.)

Instructions regarding War Diaries and Intelligence Summaries are contained in F.S. Regs., Part II and the Staff Manual respectively. Title pages will be prepared in manuscript.

Place	Date	Hour	Summary of Events and Information	Remarks and references to Appendices
ALBERT	11th April		MT No 2008 Sweeper BHANTA was struck off the strength of the section.	Demobic of W. Est.
Do.	12. 4. 13. 4. 14.		nothing to note	
Do.	15th April		Received orders to join Division in back area.	
Do.	16th April		Section left ALBERT & arrived at MARIEUX about noon. Men marched to Tn at ACHEUX & were brought into billets in the lorry.	
Do.	17 & 18		nothing to note.	
Do.	19th April		20 men under Capt. WILD to OVILLERS to work in area all received by SIALKOTE Brigade	

2353 Wt. W2544/1454 700,000 5/15 D.D.&L. A.D.S.S./Forms/C. 2118.

WAR DIARY
or
INTELLIGENCE SUMMARY.
(Erase heading not required.)

Army Form C. 2118.

Place	Date	Hour	Summary of Events and Information	Remarks and references to Appendices
MARIEUX	20th April		L/Kn. No. 587 Sweeper MANGLI has been invalided with to the Strength of the Section.	Sgt. Reed
"	21st April		Nothing to note.	Reed
"	22nd April		No. 545.322 2/Sergt. FENN, J.A. RAMC (T) has been despatched on leave to to the Royal Engineers	Reed
"	23rd "			
"	24 "			
"	25 "		nothing to note	Reed
"	26 "			
"	27 "			
"	28 "			
"	29th April		The following sweepers arrived in reinforcement from the base & were taken on the strength of the Section. PNA. 309 ABDUL RAHMAN — MT 2076 GUDHARI — MT 2053 MANGAL— MT 2029 ITWARI, & MT 66 MOLAR	Reed
"	30th April		Corpl. WILD H. Kennedy returned to duty from leave.	Sgt. Reed Capt. No. 4 (Cavalry) Section

No. 4 (Cavalry) Section

4th Cav. Div. Sanitary Sec'n.

May 1917 - June 1917.

COMMITTEE FOR THE
MEDICAL HISTORY OF THE WAR
Date 27 JUL 1917

Army Form C. 2118.

WAR DIARY
OF
INTELLIGENCE SUMMARY.
(Erase heading not required.)

Original copy for MAY 1914 appx 1.
"Medical" Serial No. 296.

Place	Date	Hour	Summary of Events and Information	Remarks and references to Appendices
				From 1st May to 30th June 1914.

SECRET

War Diary
of
Captain C. R. O'BRIEN. Indian Medical Service
Officer Commanding 4th Cavalry Sanitary Section.

from 1st May 1914 to 31st May 1914

(4th June XXIV)

3353 Wt. W2544/1454 700,000 5/15 D.D.&L. A.D.S.S./Forms/C. 2118.

Original copy MAY, 1914

WAR DIARY
or
INTELLIGENCE SUMMARY.
(Erase heading not required.)

Army Form C. 2118.

Instructions regarding War Diaries and Intelligence Summaries are contained in F. S. Regs., Part II. and the Staff Manual respectively. Title pages will be prepared in manuscript.

Place	Date	Hour	Summary of Events and Information	Remarks and references to Appendices
MARIEUX	1st May 1917		N° 545,065 P⁺ᵉ EDWARDS J.L. R.A.M.C. (T.F.) joined for duty from 9ᵗʰ Sanitary Section, 1st Cavalry Division	1st Cav. Divn. sgt. list
D°	2nd		to complete establishment	
D°	3rd		nothing to note	
D°	4th		N° MEERUT 2056 Sweeper RAM - DIAL was invalided and struck off the strength of the Section	
D°	5th			
D°	6th 7th 8th		nothing to note	
D°	9ᵗʰ		Sweepers N° MEERUT 2 HARKESH, & N° MHOW 297 NUNDOO were invalided out & struck off the strength of the section	

Army Form C. 2118.

WAR DIARY
or
INTELLIGENCE SUMMARY.
(Erase heading not required.)

Place	Date	Hour	Summary of Events and Information	Remarks and references to Appendices
MARIEUX	10.4		} nothing to note	
	11.4			
	12.4			
"	13.4		MEERUT No. 117 Sweeper CHAJJU	
			" " 116 " BHAGWANA	
			" " 39 " PERSHOD	
			Found for duty from the Indian Cavalry afore-mentioned kept in mire labour	
"	14.4		BNG. No. 18 Sweeper CHOWTHIAN was awarded 12 strokes for not erecting a dis-[?] in billet, & striking a Sweeper	
"	15.4		Received orders to move to a new area	

A 5834 Wt. W4973/M687 750,000 8/16 D. D. & L. Ltd. Forms/C.2118/13.

Army Form C. 2118.

WAR DIARY
or
INTELLIGENCE SUMMARY.
(Erase heading not required.)

Instructions regarding War Diaries and Intelligence Summaries are contained in F. S. Regs., Part II. and the Staff Manual respectively. Title pages will be prepared in manuscript.

Place	Date	Hour	Summary of Events and Information	Remarks and references to Appendices
FOUQUES	16th	that.	Lectin moved to hrs trops to view brow & Compy	No Bomb syllabus
			in an open field when here hut up howitzer	
D°	17th			
	18th		nothing to note.	
	19th			
D°	20th		B.N.G. No 14 Lucepe KEMPA has chullet to hospital to Scalie.	
	21st			
	22nd			
	23rd		nothing to note.	
	24th			
D°	25th			
	26th			

WAR DIARY
or
INTELLIGENCE SUMMARY

Army Form C. 2118.

Place	Date	Hour	Summary of Events and Information	Remarks and references to Appendices
FOURQUES	27.4.17		Troope KEMPA reported the section in discharge from Hospital	[initial] Capt [illegible]
Do	28.4.17		1 man granted 5 days leave to PARIS, handed over charge to Capt. W.F. HAWKINS R.A.M.C.	[initial]
Do	29.4.17		Nothing to note	[initial]
Do	30.4.17		M.S. 3046 PTE ROBBINS R.W. U.K. from 3/5/17 to 8/6/17.	[initial]
Do	31.4.17		BNG 14 Troope KEMPA 20 " UPPIAH Temporary duty with the mounted Brigade headquarters	[initial] Capt [illegible]

(Original)

Army Form C. 2118.

WAR DIARY
or
INTELLIGENCE SUMMARY.
(Erase heading not required.)

(SECRET.)

War Diary
of
Captain C.R. O'BRIEN, Indian Medical Service,
Officer Commanding 4th Cavalry Sanitary Section

from 1st June 1914
to 30th June 1914.

(signed) C.R. O'Brien Capt. IMS

WAR DIARY
or
INTELLIGENCE SUMMARY.

(Erase heading not required.)

Army Form C. 2118.

Place	Date	Hour	Summary of Events and Information	Remarks and references to Appendices
FOURQUES	1st June 1917		} nothing to note	
	2nd			
	3rd			
D.	4th		Sniper UPPIAH attached SIALKOTE brigade kent — another no observed by sniper GUOHAR in	Reid Burk Capt. Reid
D.	5th		Snipers KALOO, KHACHEROD, MOLAR NAYNE, & MANGA now temporarily attached for duty with hints and land parties were struck off return strength accordingly.	
D.	6th		} nothing to note.	
	7th			
	8th			
	9th			
	10th		attend Corps sniping conference	

Army Form C. 2118.

WAR DIARY
or
INTELLIGENCE SUMMARY.
(Erase heading not required.)

Instructions regarding War Diaries and Intelligence Summaries are contained in F. S. Regs., Part II. and the Staff Manual respectively. Title pages will be prepared in manuscript.

Place	Date	Hour	Summary of Events and Information	Remarks and references to Appendices
FOUQUES	11		M.T. No 2017 Lucifer BALZOUR was admitted to hospital two strength 91 return strength according to Rt. Rev.	
	12			
	13			
	14			
	15			
	16		nothing to note.	
"	17			
	18		attended County Corps. Secretary Conference	
"	19		nothing to note.	
"	20		Lucifer BALZOUR was discharged from Hospital two when in return strength according to	
"	21			
	22			
	23		nothing to note.	
	24			
	25			

WAR DIARY
or
INTELLIGENCE SUMMARY.

Army Form C. 2118.

Place	Date	Hour	Summary of Events and Information	Remarks and references to Appendices
FOURQUES	26/June		Attended Sanitary Conference at Corps head quarters.	[signed] Capt RAMC
"	27		nothing to note	
"	28		Thunderstorm with heavy rain at 7 P.M.	
"	29		} nothing to note	
"	30			[signed] Capt RAMC

Sans. Sect. — 4th Cav. Div.

COMMITTEE FOR THE
MEDICAL HISTORY OF THE WAR
Date 16 OCT. 1917

Army Form C. 2118.

Serial No. 296.

WAR DIARY
or
INTELLIGENCE SUMMARY.
(Erase heading not required.)

Original Capt. 2O'B July 1914

Instructions regarding War Diaries and Intelligence Summaries are contained in F. S. Regs., Part II. and the Staff Manual respectively. Title pages will be prepared in manuscript.

Place	Date	Hour	Summary of Events and Information	Remarks and references to Appendices

SECRET.

War Diary
of
Captain C.R. O'BRIEN Indian Medical Service
Officer Commanding 4th Cavalry Military Section
from 1st July 1914 to 31st July 1914.
(Volume XVI)

Original copy July 1917

Army Form C. 2118.

WAR DIARY
or
INTELLIGENCE SUMMARY
(Erase heading not required.)

Instructions regarding War Diaries and Intelligence Summaries are contained in F. S. Regs., Part II. and the Staff Manual respectively. Title pages will be prepared in manuscript.

Place	Date	Hour	Summary of Events and Information	Remarks and references to Appendices
FOURQUES	1 July		nothing to note.	
"	2nd		D°.	
"	3rd		Europeans KALOO, KHACHEROO, NANNE, MOLAR, MANGA returned to the reserves from temporary duty at divisional headquarters which returned to ATHIES from the Command areas	
	4th			
	5th			
	6th		nothing to note	
	7th			
	8th			
	9th			
"	10th		Europe GODARIA returned reserves from headquarters of the Rio Mounted Brigade	

Army Form C. 2118.

WAR DIARY
or
INTELLIGENCE SUMMARY.
(Erase heading not required.)

Place	Date	Hour	Summary of Events and Information	Remarks and references to Appendices
FOURGUES	1 July	11th	Proceeded on leave to the United Kingdom	
"	12th		Leave dated from 13th to 22nd July.	appld
"	13th		Nothing to note.	nil
"	14th		Indian Kaloo, Nanne, Purbhoo, Phussa, & Manga were despatched on duty with divisional headquarters & now struck off the ration strength.	nil
"	15th		Capt F. Wild R.A.M.C. was lent to 4th Army School of Sanitation at PERONNE to assist in training	nil
"	16th			
"	17th		} nothing to hark.	nil
"	18th			
"	19th			
"	21		Capt. Wild returned from leave	nil

Army Form C. 2118.

WAR DIARY
or
INTELLIGENCE SUMMARY.
(Erase heading not required.)

Instructions regarding War Diaries and Intelligence Summaries are contained in F. S. Regs., Part II. and the Staff Manual respectively. Title pages will be prepared in manuscript.

Place	Date	Hour	Summary of Events and Information	Remarks and references to Appendices
FOURQUES	21st	1 A.M.	B M S 18 Sweeper CHOWTHIAN been been found sick to SIALKOTE B.F.A. been struck off his return strength	
"	22nd		nothing to note	
"	23rd		Returned from leave — 2/Cpl J.L. EDWARDS R.A.M.C. left section to serve to the undies Army ammn	
"	24th		nothing to note	
"	25th			
"	26th		Sweeper CHOWTHIAN reported section on discharge from hospital	
"	27th		MT 24 + 66 Sweeper PAHARI & MOLAR new transfers sent to SIALKOTE C.F.A	
"	28th		nothing to note	
"	29th			
"	30th			
"	31st			

4th Res Div. Somerset

Aug 1917

COMMITTEE FOR THE
MEDICAL HISTORY OF THE WAR
Date 16 OCT. 1917

Army Form C. 2118.

Serial No. 296.

(Original date August 1914)

WAR DIARY
or
INTELLIGENCE SUMMARY.
(Erase heading not required.)

"Medical"

Instructions regarding War Diaries and Intelligence Summaries are contained in F. S. Regs., Part II. and the Staff Manual respectively. Title pages will be prepared in manuscript.

Place	Date	Hour	Summary of Events and Information	Remarks and references to Appendices

(SECRET)

War Diary
of
Lt-Colonel C. R. O'BRIEN
Officer Commanding 4th Cavalry Sanitary Section

(From 1st August 1914 to 31st August 1914)

Volume XXVII

(Original) AUGUST 1917

WAR DIARY
or
INTELLIGENCE SUMMARY.
(Erase heading not required.)

Army Form C. 2118.

Instructions regarding War Diaries and Intelligence Summaries are contained in F.S. Regs., Part II. and the Staff Manual respectively. Title pages will be prepared in manuscript.

Place	Date	Hour	Summary of Events and Information	Remarks and references to Appendices
FOURDUES	August 1917 1		nothing of note all cloudy day with heavy wind & rain	
do	2		nothing to note. Rained. shelled all night	nil
do	3		Cpl. CLINCH R.A.M.C. & Pte DYER left for BAYEUX for 5 days leave. My private servant AHMED HOSSEIN despatched from recruit via MARSEILLES en route to INDIA	nil
do	4		nothing to note	nil
do	5		M/66 Sweeper MOLAR returned to duty after being discharged from hospital	nil
do	6		} nothing to note	nil
	7			
do	8			

Army Form C. 2118.

WAR DIARY
or
INTELLIGENCE SUMMARY.
(Erase heading not required.)

Instructions regarding War Diaries and Intelligence Summaries are contained in F. S. Regs., Part II. and the Staff Manual respectively. Title pages will be prepared in manuscript.

Place	Date	Hour	Summary of Events and Information	Remarks and references to Appendices
FOURQUES	9 August		Capt. CLINCH & Pte DYER returned from 5 days leave at CAYEUX	Chen Divr syl Rest
"	10 "			
"	11 "			
"	12 "		2nd Army to rule	
"	13 "			
"	14 "			nil
"	15 "		BNG/18 Lascars CHOWTHIAN was admitted to hospital & struck off return strength.	nil
"	16 "		} nothing to rule.	
"	17 "			
"	18 "		Capt. WILD & Capt. EDWARDS with 12 men each left for JEANCOURT & VADENCOURT respectively to dig cable trenches for the advanced dressing stations there	ref'd

Army Form C. 2118.

WAR DIARY
or
INTELLIGENCE SUMMARY.
(Erase heading not required.)

Instructions regarding War Diaries and Intelligence Summaries are contained in F.S. Regs., Part II. and the Staff Manual respectively. Title pages will be prepared in manuscript.

Place	Date	Hour	Summary of Events and Information	Remarks and references to Appendices
FOURQUES	1917 August		nothing to note	
"	20th		Pte ROBBINS A.S.C. depended on 5 days leave to PARIS	Under syphilis
"	21st		Sweeper CHOWTHIAN opened the wound in discharge from hospital	
"	22nd		Sweepers KRISHNASWAMY, MARIAN, YESSAIYH & MUMSWAMY (N°63) had under knees at night for breaking a lantern & [illeg] in bullets	
"	23rd		Sweepers KRISHNASWAMY & MARIAN received 12 stripes each — the cause for assaulting a comrade & the little in hurry GANJA in his possession. Jemadar KALOO & 14 sweepers returned to the section lines. Previous headquarters were replaced by 16 others.	

As834 Wt.W4973/M687 750,000 8/16 I.D.&L. Ltd. Forms/C.2118/13.

WAR DIARY
or
INTELLIGENCE SUMMARY.

Army Form C. 2118.

Place	Date	Hour	Summary of Events and Information	Remarks and references to Appendices
FOURQUES	24 August		Cpl. CLINCH R.A.M.C. was granted leave to the United Kingdom from this date	
"	25 "		} nothing to note	
"	26 "			
"	27 "		Received intimation that Cpl. CLINCH & Pte EDWARDS were promoted acting Sergeant & Corporal respectively. Promotion to date from 27/5/17	
"	28 "		Pte ROBBINS returned from PARIS leave having been detained on the return journey } nothing to note	
"	29 "			
"	30 "			
"	31 "		Sweeper KRISHNASWAMY received 10 strokes in respect Ganja in a parcel from INDIA the sentence was carried out by the A.P.M.	

4th Aus. Div. Sanitary Section

COMMITTEE FOR THE
MEDICAL HISTORY OF THE WAR
Date 12 DEC. 1917

ORIGINAL

Army Form C. 2118.

Serial No. 206

WAR DIARY
INTELLIGENCE SUMMARY
(Erase heading not required.)

Place	Date	Hour	Summary of Events and Information	Remarks and references to Appendices

(SECRET)

War Diary

of

No 5 Coy C.R. O'BRIEN under Middx Divn

Officer Commanding 1st Cavalry Divisn Base Depot

(from 1st Oct 1914 to 3rd Feb 1915)

Appdx XXVII

Army Form C. 2118.

WAR DIARY
or
INTELLIGENCE SUMMARY.
(Erase heading not required.)

Place	Date	Hour	Summary of Events and Information	Remarks and references to Appendices
FOUQUES	October 1		Nothing to note.	
	2			
"	3		Staff Sergt J HASELL R.A.M.C. proceeded on ten days leave to the United Kingdom	
	4		Nothing to note.	
"	5			
"	6		Sergt H.G. CLINCH. R.A.M.C.(T) returned from leave to the United Kingdom	
	7			
	8			
	9			
	10		Nothing to note.	
	11			
	12			
	13			
	14			

Army Form C. 2118.

WAR DIARY
or
INTELLIGENCE SUMMARY.
(Erase heading not required.)

Instructions regarding War Diaries and Intelligence Summaries are contained in F. S. Regs., Part II. and the Staff Manual respectively. Title pages will be prepared in manuscript.

Place	Date	Hour	Summary of Events and Information	Remarks and references to Appendices
FOURGES	15th October		nothing to note	
Do	16th		By order of the A.D.M.S Sweeper MARIKAN AETENALLY was temporarily transferred to the Princes Battalion. Private L. WATSON A.S.C (M.T) was admitted to AMBALLA C.F.A. was struck off the ration strength accordingly.	R.Gun cpl Und Und
Do	17th		Nothing to note	Und
Do	18th		Staff Serg. HASELL R.A.M.C. returned from leave to the United Kingdom having been detained ill. No change in ranks.	Und
Do	19th		nothing to note	Und
Do	20th		Sweeper BANSI was admitted sick to AMBALLA C.F.A	Und

Army Form C. 2118.

WAR DIARY
or
INTELLIGENCE SUMMARY.
(Erase heading not required.)

Instructions regarding War Diaries and Intelligence Summaries are contained in F. S. Regs., Part II. and the Staff Manual respectively. Title pages will be prepared in manuscript.

Place	Date	Hour	Summary of Events and Information	Remarks and references to Appendices
FOURQUES	21		M2 032268 Pte ERIBETTA J. A.S.C.(M.T.) proceeded from 4th Cavalry Supply column with FORD Box car had been detached to Head quarters 4th C.D. returned to unit	
"	22		Nothing to note	
"	23		Sweeper CHAJJU was transferred with L. ANIBALLA 62A L Head quarters 4th C.D.	
			M2 095795 Pte DOBBIE A. A.S.C.(M.T.) proceeded from 4th Cavalry Supply column with trailer cycle & tools &c. had been attached to Head quarters 4th C.D.	
"	24		Nothing to note.	
"	25		Private WATSON K. A.S.C.(M.T.) was discharged from Hospital & returned to strength	
"	26		Nothing to note.	
"	27			
"	28			
"	29			
"	31			

E. [signature]
Capt R.H.C.
Commanding
4th No 4 (Cavalry) Sanitary Section

4 Cav. Sanitary Section.

Oct. 1917

COMMITTEE FOR THE
MEDICAL HISTORY OF THE WAR
Date -8 FEB. 1918

(ORIGINAL COPY - OCTOBER 1914)

Army Form C. 2118

WAR DIARY
or
INTELLIGENCE SUMMARY.
(Erase heading not required.)

(SECRET.)

WAR DIARY

of

Captn. C.R. O'BRIEN Indian Medical Service
Officer Commanding 4th Wessex Sanitary Section

from 1st October 1914 to 31st October 1914

(Volume XIX.)

WAR DIARY
or
INTELLIGENCE SUMMARY.

Army Form C. 2118.

Place	Date	Hour	Summary of Events and Information	Remarks and references to Appendices
FOURQUES	1st Oct/17		Sweeper MARIKAN & AETENALLY rejoined the section having been in hospital. One lorry of the 4th Div Mounted Battalion chain	
do	2nd		1 Chauffer Louis BANSI was discharged from hospital and taken on ration strength.	
do	3rd		Pte WATSON A.S.C. (M.T.) was granted leave to the United Kingdom from date to 13th inclusive	
do	4th		} nothing to note	
do	5th			
do	6th			
do	7th		Capt. WILD R.A.M.C. Pte OVER 17th Sheen were granted leave to the United Kingdom from date to the 17th inclusive	
do	8th		Pte DOBBIE proceed the orders with train transport do. A 2/Lt DAVIS & Pte ROBBINS have transferred to the supply column to Pannels in Laon to.	

WAR DIARY
or
INTELLIGENCE SUMMARY.

Army Form C. 2118.

Place	Date	Hour	Summary of Events and Information	Remarks and references to Appendices
FOURAGES	9th Oct			
	10th		Nothing to note	
	11th			
	12th		Shiny S.W. gale with hard squalls blowing all day	
	13th		Jennifer Sweeper BANSI sent to S.Y.A. L.W. Field Ambulance continued	
	14th		PTE WATSON A.S.O. (M.T.) returned from 10 days leave to the United Kingdom; from leave on return strength.	
	15th		Nothing to note	
	16th		Jennifer Sweeper BANSI has discharged to hospital now taken on strength	
	17th		Nothing to note. A.D.M.S. Sweeper NETANAHI GODAR	
	18th		Reported to the A.D.M.S. the IUEROWLES has taken place in a temporary manner	

Army Form C. 2118.

WAR DIARY
or
INTELLIGENCE SUMMARY.
(Erase heading not required.)

Place	Date	Hour	Summary of Events and Information	Remarks and references to Appendices
FOURQUES	19th October		Lieut. WILD R.A.M.C. returned from leave to the United Kingdom.	
Do	20th		Six sweepers were temporarily transferred to work at Divisional Headquarters by order of the A.D.M.S.	
Do	21st		Nothing to note.	
Do	22nd		Pte DYER 17th Lancer attached Sam team to the "Lowden King Sam" having had an extension of 3 days from the two officers.	
Do	23rd		One Irish N.C.O., Corp. WILLIS R.A.M.C. sent for further Operation was sent to hospital from here to Corps Corps W.R., BEAUQUESNE. 10 N.P.M's Corp Cmdt for duty here.	
Do	24th		Capt. O'Brien proceeded on one months leave to England. Temporary command of unit is assumed by Capt. R.M. LANG R.A.M.C Ambulance H.G. a/c	

Army Form C. 2118.

WAR DIARY
or
INTELLIGENCE SUMMARY.
(Erase heading not required.)

Instructions regarding War Diaries and Intelligence Summaries are contained in F. S. Regs., Part II. and the Staff Manual respectively. Title pages will be prepared in manuscript.

Place	Date	Hour	Summary of Events and Information	Remarks and references to Appendices
FOURDRES	25th Oct/A		Pte Gains & Pte M.S. reported unit from leave to England.	
	26th		Six sweepers reported return from Div. H.Q. where they had been on temporary duty. Nothing to record.	
	27th		British N.C.O. and four men returned from Can. Corps H.Q. Nothing to record.	
	28th			
	29th		Sgt Clinch Rance and three sweepers proceeded to the Divisional Training School D.A.O.U.R.S. for duty. Nothing to report.	
	31st		Ruturg Col F Rhone	
			Acting O.C. 2nd Can Sanitary Section.	

4th Div. Sanitary Section.

Nov. 1917

COMMITTEE FOR THE
MEDICAL HISTORY OF THE WAR
Date -8 FEB. 1918

WAR DIARY
or
INTELLIGENCE SUMMARY.
(Erase heading not required.)

Army Form C. 2118.

(SECRET)

War Diary

of

Lieut. Col. C.R. O'BRIEN

Officer Commanding 1st Cavalry Brigade Signal Troop

From 1st November 1914 to 30th November 1914

W. Browne Lt.Col.

November 1914

Army Form C. 2118.

WAR DIARY
or
INTELLIGENCE SUMMARY.
(Erase heading not required.)

Place	Date	Hour	Summary of Events and Information	Remarks and references to Appendices
FOURQUES	Nov. 1917 1st		nothing to record	
"	2nd		Capt. EDWARDS R.A.M.C proceeded on 3 days leave to DESVRES. PAS-DE-CALAIS. Two Sweepers detailed for Sanitary duties under the working party. BRIE Chatan. Pte MULDOWNEY A.S.C up for 14 days leave to England. Sweeper MOLAR invalided sick to AMBALA G.F.A.	D. Brian Cpl died
"	3rd		Two Sweepers KACHERU & BHAGWANA arrived as reinforcements from Indian Base depot	
"	4th		} nothing to record	
"	5th			
"	6th		Capt. EDWARDS arrived from leave to DESVRES etc.	
"	7th		} nothing to report	
"	8th			

WAR DIARY
or
INTELLIGENCE SUMMARY
(Erase heading not required.)

Army Form C. 2118.

Place	Date	Hour	Summary of Events and Information	Remarks and references to Appendices
FOURDES	Nov 1917 9th		Two Sweepers LALU & BISHNA AHE 1 ward Br duty. Unm admitted hos depot	
"	10th		Two Sweeper attached for duty at unmounted Headquarters returned duties	
"	11th		} nothing to record	
"	12th			
"	13th			
"	14th			
"	15th			
"	16th		Two Sweepers returned from duty at BRIE Station without to record	
"	17th		Two Sweepers MAULA + BHIKA arrived & reinforced	
"	18th		Lieut Col MOLDOWNEY returned from leave & took over the Regt	
"	19th		Capt C.R O'BRIEN I.M.S in rear from leave reported took over command of the unit. Sweeper KHANA passed the unit & a new providential	

Army Form C. 2118.

WAR DIARY
or
INTELLIGENCE SUMMARY.
(Erase heading not required.)

Place	Date	Hour	Summary of Events and Information	Remarks and references to Appendices
FOURQUES	Nov 20		Nothing to note.	
Do	21		The Division less B. ECHELON moved to concentration area about 9 A.M.	
Do	22		Nothing to note.	
Do	23		The division returned to billets from concentration area	
Do	24		Troops PAOSE were admitted to hospital & church at the strength. The division moved up to concentration in the evening	
Do	25 N	}		
	26 N		Nothing to note.	
	27 N			
	28 N			
	29 N			
Do	30 N		VILLERS FAUCON entrance	
			A relief of the division moved into action	

ORIGINAL DECEMBER 1917

Army Form C. 2118.

WAR DIARY
or
INTELLIGENCE SUMMARY. Medical
(Erase heading not required.)

292

SECRET.
War Diary
of
Walter C.R. O'Brien
Officer Commanding 2nd Wessex Casualty Clearing Station
France. December 1917.
XXVI

COMMITTEE FOR THE
MEDICAL HISTORY OF THE WAR
Date 12 JUL 1920

Dec. 1917

Army Form C. 2118.

WAR DIARY
or
INTELLIGENCE SUMMARY.

(Erase heading not required.)

Instructions regarding War Diaries and Intelligence Summaries are contained in F. S. Regs., Part II. and the Staff Manual respectively. Title pages will be prepared in manuscript.

Place	Date	Hour	Summary of Events and Information	Remarks and references to Appendices
FOUADIES	1st December			
do	2nd		nothing to note. One Officer the Division returned to unit.	cpt sent
do	3rd		nothing to note	
do	4th			
do	5th		Under orders from the A.D.M.S. Sniper KACHERU JODHPUR O.7.A being unfit to men transferred to estb detachment	
do	6th		nothing to note	
do	7th			
do	8th		Sniper BHAGIA arrived from here as a reinforcement has taken on strength	
do	9th			
do	10th		nothing to report	
do	11th			
do	12th		Sniper MANGAT reported sick now admitted to hospital	
do	13th		Under orders from the A.D.M.S. Sniper BAKSHI & MANGAT were transferred to temporary duty to the LUCKNOW C.C.S.	

WAR DIARY
or
INTELLIGENCE SUMMARY.
(Erase heading not required.)

Army Form C. 2118.

Place	Date	Hour	Summary of Events and Information	Remarks and references to Appendices
FOURQUES	14 December		} nothing to report	
	15			
	16			
"	17 "		froze all day	
			snow fell heavily throughout the night	
"	18 "			
	19 "		} Frost continues	
"	20 "			
	21 "			
	22 "			
	23 "			
"	24 "		Thawing slightly	
	25 "		Thawed throughout the day, but froze again at night	
"	26 "		Snow fell again during the night	
	27 "			
"	28 "		} Continues to freeze. Nothing else to report	
	29 "			
	30 "			
	31 "			

(Original January 1916) **WAR DIARY** or **INTELLIGENCE SUMMARY**. Army Form C.2118.

Medical / 4 Cav: Saw: &c

296

War Diary

SECRET

War Diary
of
CAPT. C.R. O'BRIEN ..... I.M.S.
Officer Commanding 4th Cavalry Sanatory [?]
from 1st January 1918 to 31st January 1918.

Volume XXXII

Place	Date	Hour	Summary of Events and Information	Remarks and references to Appendices
	January			

WAR DIARY
or
INTELLIGENCE SUMMARY.
(Erase heading not required.)

Army Form C. 2118.

Place	Date	Hour	Summary of Events and Information	Remarks and references to Appendices
FOUR QUES	1st January 1918		Took over charge of No. 5 & 9 Sanitary Sections in addition to my own duties. Pte Cpl. WHITE R.A.M.C.(T) Granted leave to Eire to the United Kingdom	
"	2nd		Nothing to record	
"	3rd			
"	4th			
"	5th		Sweeper KHANA was invalided sick & now struck off strength of Section	
"	6th			
"	7th		Nothing to record	
"	8th			
"	9th		Sapper ASTENALLY was invalided sick now struck off the strength of the Section	
"	10th		Nothing to record	
"	11th			
"	12th		Dr DOBBIE A.S.C. (M.T) was transferred to G.H.Q. Sy. Sec. Struck off strength of Section	

WAR DIARY
or
INTELLIGENCE SUMMARY.
(Erase heading not required.)

Place	Date	Hour	Summary of Events and Information	Remarks and references to Appendices
FOURQUES	13 January		nothing to record	
"	14 "		M.T/96 Sweeper KHANA was admitted to the C.C.S. & BN4/19 Sweeper BAKSHI was evacuated sick to no 1 base & struck off the strength of the section	
"	15 "		nothing to record	
"	16 "		LKN/584 / Jemadar Sweeper BANSI + PNA/176 Sweeper BESHAR have evacuated sick to AMBALA C.F.A	
"	17 "		nothing to date	
"	18 "		Handed over command of No 59 Sanitary Section to Capt WHITE R.A.M.C on his return from leave M0/096.795 Pte DOBBIE T A.S.C (M.T) reported for duty from G.H.Q Supply column.	
"	19 " 20 " 21 " 22 " 23 "		nothing to record	

WAR DIARY
or
INTELLIGENCE SUMMARY.
(Erase heading not required.)

Place	Date	Hour	Summary of Events and Information	Remarks and references to Appendices
FOURQUES	24 January		Proceeded on six days leave to PARIS.	Nil
"	25 "		Nothing to report.	Nil
"	26 "		Sergt. CLINCH R.A.M.C. (T) & 3 Conscripts returned to duty from Divisional School.	Nil
"	27 "		} Nothing to report.	
"	28 "			
"	29 "			
"	30 "		Returned from leave to PARIS.	
"	31 "		Nothing to report.	W. Rhea Capt. RAMC M

ORIGINAL (FEBRUARY 1918)

Army Form C. 2118.
No. 296

WAR DIARY
or
INTELLIGENCE SUMMARY.
(Erase heading not required.)

SECRET.

War Diary
of
Officer Commanding No 1 Canadian Sanitary Section
from 1st February 1918 to 28th February 1918.

Volume XXXIII

COMMITTEE
MEDICAL
12 JUL 1918

Army Form C. 2118.

WAR DIARY
or
INTELLIGENCE SUMMARY.
(Erase heading not required.)

Instructions regarding War Diaries and Intelligence Summaries are contained in F. S. Regs., Part II. and the Staff Manual respectively. Title pages will be prepared in manuscript.

Place	Date	Hour	Summary of Events and Information	Remarks and references to Appendices
FOURQUES	1st February 1915		nothing to record.	
Do	2nd		Under orders from A.D.M.S. two officers were detailed for temporary duty with head quarters this morning. Brigade at HEAVILLY	
Do	3rd		nothing to record	
Do	4th			
	5th		nothing to record	
Do	6th		attached body under Lieut. Serg. CLINCH R.A.M.C. sent to new billetting area at SALEUX.	
Do	7th		Remainder of section moved into new billetting area at SALEUX.	
SALEUX	8th		nothing to note.	
Do	9th		2 officers detailed for temporary duty at Divisional head quarters	
Do	10th			
	11th		} nothing to record	
	12th			
	13th			
	14th			

Army Form C. 2118.

WAR DIARY
or
INTELLIGENCE SUMMARY.
(Erase heading not required.)

Instructions regarding War Diaries and Intelligence Summaries are contained in F. S. Regs., Part II. and the Staff Manual respectively. Title pages will be prepared in manuscript.

Place	Date	Hour	Summary of Events and Information	Remarks and references to Appendices
BAKLOH	15th		One of the Sis Sweepers temporarily detached to dispensary. Sweeper returned & was taken on strength.	
"	16th			
"	17th		Nothing to record	
"			Sweeper ABDUL RAHMAN was invalided back to his home returned & taken on strength.	
"	18th		Recovery boy sweeper temporarily detached returned once here on return strength still absent	
"	19th			
"	20th		Nothing to record	
"	21st			
"	23rd		Sweeper was ordered to be dispensary attached to AMBALA C.H.H. I proceeded on 14 days leave to the U.K. handing over to Capt. HAWKINS. R.A.M.C.	

Army Form C. 2118.

WAR DIARY
or
INTELLIGENCE SUMMARY.
(Erase heading not required.)

Place	Date	Hour	Summary of Events and Information	Remarks and references to Appendices
SALEUX	February 23rd		Command of Section taken over from Capt. Hawkins R.A.M.C. by Lieut. Sutherland R.A.M.C. Jemadar Sweeper BANSI needs to Sweepers on being shown at the strength.	
"	24th		Sweeper GIN furnished Jemadar Sweeper with Ry. work sheets from 24-1-18.	
"	25th "		History of record	
"	26th "		Corporal WILD R.A.M.C.	Grantes 14 days leave to U.K.
"	27th "		Pte. DYER 17th Lancers	
			Sergt. OSBORNE R.A.M.C.	Joined for duty 27/2/18 from 3rd Cav. Saint Sec.
			" HODGES "	
			Cpl. GATLAND "	
"	28th "		Jemadar Sweeper GIN and Chayen left to join L.E.F.A for overseas.	

A.J. Sutherland /Lt. R.A.M.C.
to O/C 4th Cav. San Sec.

A5834 Wt. W4973/M687 750,000 8/16 D. D. & L. Ltd. Forms/C.2118/13.

WAR DIARY or INTELLIGENCE SUMMARY

Army Form C. 2118.

Title pages March 1st to 21st 1918.

HQ Mhow Cav Bde

Place	Date	Hour	Summary of Events and Information	Remarks and references to Appendices
POIX	MARCH 1918 1st		Bde Hd. moved from COURCELLES to POIX.	
		1 pm	Following entrained SALEUX for TARANTO. 1 B.O. 36 I.O.Rs. 3 Ft.Clth osse.	
			& 36 I.O.Rs. 57 O.Rs. & 6 animals Ambl Cav. Fd Aml & 4 BOR. Farriers MHow M&S 24	M
	2nd	11:30 am	1 B.O. 57 O.Rs. & 6 animals Ambl Cav. Fd Aml & 4 BOR. Farriers MHow M&S 24	
			SALEUX for TARANTO.	
	3rd		16 horses from 2nd Lancers & 52 horses from 38th C.I.H. transferred to Luckn Bde to complete them prior to departure for MARSEILLES.	SCH
	4th		12 horses transferred from Dvn S&Q to 2nd Lancers to replace above.	SCH
	6th		33 horses transferred from Bde H Q + Signal Sectn to 2nd Lancers	SCH
	7th		2nd Lancers entrained SALEUX for MARSEILLES	BGH
	8th		38th C.I.H., details of Bde H.Q. and M.V.S. entrained SALEUX for MARSEILLES	SCH

S.C. Harvey Capt.
for Bde Major
Mhow Cav. Bde

12th	Training under Squadron arrangements.
13th	Presentations of medals awarded to XX 2 B.O., 1 W.O. and 7 O.R.
16th	Training under Squadron arrangements. Reinforcements joined from Base. 3 B.O.
	-:- -:- -:- 5 animals.
17th	17 R.i transferred to 2nd L. & M.G.Sqdn.
	-:-
18th - 22nd	to complete them to War Establishment. - 2 O.R. joined from Base.
22nd	Exercise under Squadron arrangements.
23rd	6 chargers and 3 O.R. joined from Base as reinforcements.
to 31st	Training under Squadron arrangements.
	-:-

23rd to 31st Throughout the month, working parties of 2 B.O. & 200 O.R. furnished for trench work at BIHECOURT & JEANCOURT. 1 Party - 1 B.O. & 95 o.r, at HERVILLY.

=*=*=*=*=*=*=*=*=*=*=*=*=*=*=